HOME L ANCIENT GREECE

MELANIE ANN APEL

ROSEN CLASSROOM
PRIMARY SOURCE

Rosen Classroom Books & Materials

New York

To Michael and Hayden, Mom, Dad, and Mindy, with whom I share not only my home but my life

Published in 2004 by The Rosen Publishing Group, Inc.
29 East 21st Street, New York, NY 10010

First Edition

Editor: Joanne Randolph
Book Design: Michael DeGuzman
Layout Design: Kim Sonsky
Photo Researcher: Peter Tomlinson

Cover (center) The Art Archive/Archaeological Museum Istanbul/Dagli Orti; cover (left), pp. 4 (right), 11 (left), 12 (right), 16 (left), 19 Erich Lessing/Art Resource, NY; p. 4 (left) The Art Archive/Kanellopoulos Museum Athens/Dagli Orti; p. 7 © Ruggero Vanni/CORBIS; p. 7 (inset) AKG London/Peter Connolly; p. 8 The Art Archive/Dagli Orti; pp. 11 (right), 20 (left) Réunion des Musées Nationaux/Art Resource, NY; pp. 12 (left), 20 (right) The Art Archive/Musée du Louvre Paris/Dagli Orti; p. 15 (left) The Art Archive /National Archaeological Museum Athens/Dagli Orti; p. 15 (right) The Art Archive/Agora Museum Athens/Dagli Orti; p. 16 (right) © Gianni Dagli Orti/CORBIS.

Apel, Melanie Ann.
Home life in ancient Greece / Melanie Ann Apel.
   v. cm.—(Primary sources of ancient civilizations. Greece)
Includes bibliographical references and index.
Contents: The family—Communities—The Greek house—Greek marriage—Women's role in the home—Slavery—Greek fashion—Greek food—Children in Ancient Greece—Sports and entertainment.
   ISBN 0-8239-6772-7 (library binding)—ISBN 0-8239-8940-2 (paperback)
1. Greece—Social life and customs—Juvenile literature. [1. Greece—Social life and customs—To 146 B.C. 2. Family—Greece.] I. Title. II. Series.
   DF91 .A64 2004
   938—dc21   2003000741

Manufactured in the United States of America

Contents

A mother and her child are shown holding hands in this relief carving. On average, Greek women had about five children, though some had as many as ten.

The Family

Family served as the basis of ancient Greek civilization. Every family was responsible for taking care of itself and providing food and shelter for its members. Each family member felt a sense of belonging. The older family members taught the younger generations lessons about the traditions of the family and ancient Greek culture. Greeks used the word *oikos* to describe the family unit, which included close relatives, slaves, and the house in which all the members of the household lived. Oikos was also the word for the hearth, where cooking was done. The family plot of land, called the *kleros*, was passed down from father to son.

Meleager and his son Parthenopaeus say good-bye to their family before leaving to hunt in this scene painted on pottery. Notice the woman and the older man in the image. The whole extended family might live in the same home.

Communities

Although there were major differences among the lifestyles of Greeks in different city-states, such as Sparta and Athens, many aspects of daily life were very much the same. Ancient Greeks shared a strong sense of community. People viewed their community as an extended family. Within the community people lived in single-family houses or apartment buildings, depending on how much money they had. Homes, public buildings, and temples were built around the agora, or town center. Every day people met and shopped in the agora for food or other goods. Some people, especially those who owned farms, lived outside town.

A stoa, which bordered the agora, had columns, a roof, and a wall on one side. It provided shelter from rain or sun and served as a gathering place. Inset: People got freshwater from the agora's springhouse. ▶

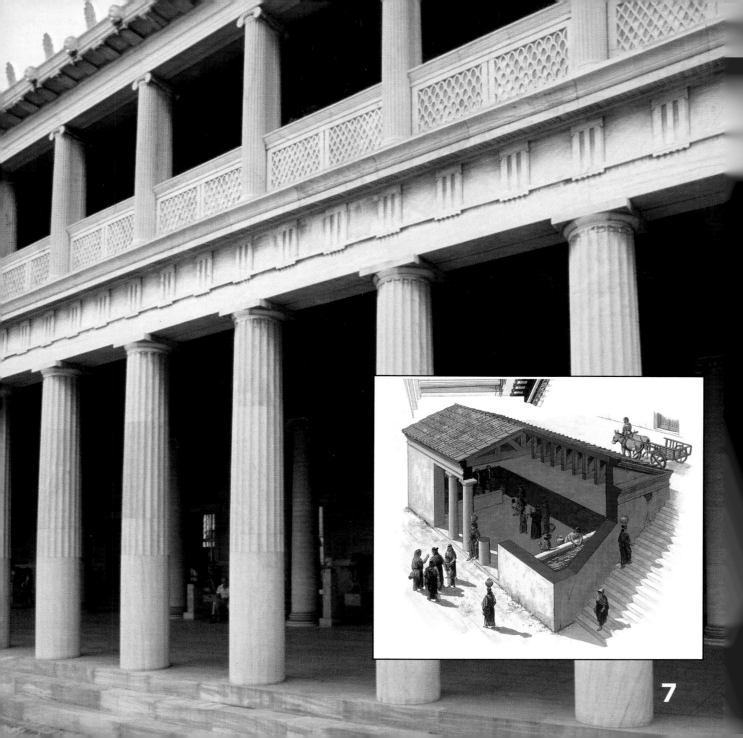

The Greek House

Greek houses varied in size depending on their location and the families living in them. Most homes had only one door and small windows. Each had bedrooms and a kitchen. Larger homes might have other rooms and storage space. Furniture was simple. Homes belonging to wealthier families might have floors covered in decorative mosaics. Sometimes the walls were painted with colorful scenes that told stories. In the center of each house was an open courtyard, which had a small altar. The family members used the altar daily for praying and making private sacrifices to their gods. Each house also had a room, called the *andron*, used only by the men.

◀ *Shown are the ruins of a home located in Akrotiri, near Thera, Greece. Notice the windows and the thickness of the walls of this home, which was destroyed by a volcanic eruption sometime around 1500 B.C.*

Greek Marriage

Marriage was an important part of ancient Greek culture, and it was expected of all young people. Men usually got married when they were in their late twenties or early thirties. The women were younger, usually in their mid to late teens. It was usually the father's task to choose whom his children married. This was an important job for the father, because the future of his family relied on male heirs. If the father had no sons of his own, he had to choose for his daughters men whom he could trust as male heirs to run his property. Once married, a woman was expected to have children, especially boys who could work and inherit, or take over, their father's land.

In this scene painted on pottery, a Greek bride prepares for her wedding. Before the ceremony, the bride took a bath in water that had been brought to her home from a holy spring. This bath marked the start of her new life as a wife.

In this scene painted on pottery, a couple is being married. Following a wedding ceremony a feast was held in the bride's parents' home. That night, guests formed a procession to take the bride and groom to their new home.

Above: *Women from the late fifth century* B.C. *are spinning thread from wool in this scene on pottery.*

Right: *Ancient Greek women spent a lot of time spinning threads or yarn into cloth, as shown on this container.*

Women's Role in the Home

Ancient Greek society was paternalistic, or ruled by men. Men could be citizens and could participate in the government. Women could not. Women were taught from an early age that their role in life was to marry, have children, and take care of the house. Women also worked in the fields, harvesting olives, fruits, and vegetables. Although men dominated life in general, women dominated home life. The woman raised the children, made the family's clothing, and managed the household and the slaves. Spartan women could exercise, because Spartan men felt it would help the women to have stronger babies. Unless there was a religious event, however, most women went out only to visit other women or to shop at the agora.

Slavery

Almost every Greek family owned slaves. Slaves were people who were considered property. They did not have any legal rights. Slaves worked as servants and laborers. Female slaves worked as household servants. They cooked, cleaned, and fetched water for the house. In the fifth century B.C., it is believed that there were about 100,000 slaves in Attica, a region near Athens. This would have been about twice the amount of free citizens in Attica. Many of these Attic slaves worked long, hard hours in the silver mines. There were no laws to make slave owners treat their slaves well. Occasionally, owners paid their slaves a small amount of money for their work. Some slaves saved this money and bought their freedom. However, slaves could never become citizens.

Household servants were responsible for going to the springhouse or another water source to fetch water for the home. A servant is shown carrying water on this oil flask, done in the black-figure style.

In this relief carved from stone between 380 and 370 B.C., a woman is seated with her slave standing in front of her.

In this painting on pottery, cloth merchants, or sellers, work at weighing bales of cloth. Weighing cloth helped merchants to establish its price.

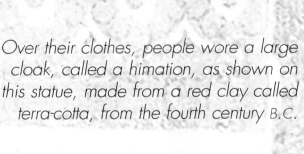

Over their clothes, people wore a large cloak, called a himation, as shown on this statue, made from a red clay called terra-cotta, from the fourth century B.C.

Greek Fashion

Ancient Greek clothing was made of linen, wool, and sometimes silk. Women spent a great deal of time making cloth for clothing. They cleaned wool or plant fibers and then dyed them bright colors, such as blue, pink, purple, and yellow. They then spun the fibers into yarn, which was woven into cloth on a loom. Women from poorer families sold their cloth at the agora. Men, women, and children dressed basically alike. Everyone wore skirts, though of different styles, lengths, and patterns. People either went barefoot or wore leather sandals or boots. Some men wore a tunic, over which they might wear a wool cloak. Women wore ankle-length dresses. Made of a large piece of fabric, the dress was wrapped around the body and was either pinned or belted.

Greek Food

Ancient Greeks ate what the land provided. Staples were grains such as barley and wheat, which were made into breads and porridge, and items made from olives and grapes, such as olive oil and wine. People ate vegetables and legumes such as chickpeas, beans, and lentils, herbs from their gardens, fish, and fruits, such as apples, grapes, pears, and pomegranates. Many farms had goats, which provided milk and cheese. The Greeks rarely ate meat, except on special days. Fish was the more common choice. People went out in their wooden fishing boats and caught octopus, squid, tuna, sturgeon, shellfish, and mackerel using spears and nets.

Top: *In this banquet scene, men dine on foods such as bread, fish, and grapes, and drink wine.* ▶

Women made bread and porridges by grinding their cereal grains into flour. This statue shows a woman working with dough for bread.

19

A school scene is shown on this cup, which was made sometime between 460 and 450 B.C.

Boys learned to read the laws, memorize and recite long works of poetry, write, and play music. This statue shows a man writing on a tablet with a special pen called a stylus. Boys in school would have practiced their lessons using a waxed tablet and a stylus as well.

Children in Ancient Greece

Greeks met the birth of a child, especially a boy, with great celebration. Children played with clay or fabric dolls. They also played with toys such as rattles, board games, and balls. By the age of 12 or 13, children were considered adults. At this age, girls prepared to get married. To mark this passage, they brought their toys to the temple and offered them to the gods.

Around age seven, boys from wealthy families went to school. Boys learned to read, write, and play music. Boys were also taught philosophy, horsemanship, athletics, public speaking, and hunting. Girls did not go to school. Their mothers taught them to care for children, run a home, spin thread, weave cloth, and cook. Some girls also learned to read, write, play music, and dance.

Sports and Entertainment

   Sports and entertainment were important to ancient Greeks. From childhood, ancient Greeks trained for regularly held competitions, called *agones*. Each town had a gymnasium, or sports center, and a stadium. Wrestling, the discus throw, boxing, and the long jump were among the first sports practiced. The most popular event was the footrace. The most famous athletic competition in the world, the Olympic Games, began in ancient Greece. These games were held every four years for several days at Olympia, the place where people went to worship the god Zeus. Winners of the games were celebrated as heroes. Of all the things that have endured from ancient Greece, it is perhaps the Olympic Games that have been enjoyed the most by people worldwide.

Glossary

agora (A-guh-ruh) A market in ancient Greece.

andron (AN-dron) A room, filled with couches, cushions, and oil lamps, in which men entertained guests and hosted parties called symposia.

city-states (SIH-tee STAYTS) Independent states made up of a city and its surrounding areas.

competitions (kom-pih-TIH-shinz) Games or tests.

culture (KUL-chur) The beliefs, practices, and arts of a group of people.

discus (DIS-kis) A circular disk that is thrown.

dominated (DAH-muh-nayt-id) Ruled over or stood above all others.

gymnasium (jim-NAY-zee-um) A sports center in ancient Greece.

hearth (HARTH) The floor of a fireplace or the space in front of it.

legal (LEE-gul) Allowed by the law.

mosaics (moh-ZAY-iks) Pictures made by fitting together small pieces of stone, glass, or tile and cementing them in place.

oikos (OY-kos) The family and its property and slaves.

paternalistic (puh-ter-nul-IS-tik) Centered on men.

philosophy (fih-LAH-suh-fee) A system of thought that tries to understand the nature of that which is real.

traditions (truh-DIH-shunz) Ways of doing things that have been passed down over time.

tunic (TOO-nik) A long, loose shirt.

Index

Primary Sources

Cover. Banqueting scene. Relief. Sixth century B.C. Greek Archaic Period. Thassos, Greece. Archaeological Museum, Istanbul. **Inset.** Wedding preparations on red-figure nuptial vase. Mid–fifth century B.C. Musée du Louvre. Paris, France. **Page 4. Bottom.** Meleager and son Parthenopaeus say good-bye to their family before leaving to hunt. Red-figure chalice krater. 420 B.C. Classical Greek Period. By the Dinos Painter. Kanellopoulos Museum, Athens, Greece. **Page 7.** Agora of Athens: Stoa of Attalus. Seventh century B.C. **Page 8.** Ruins at Akrotiri, near Thera, Greece. The destruction of this city is believed to have given rise to the Atlantis myth. These ruins were covered in ash and pumice from a volcanic eruption that dates from about 1500 B.C. **Page 11. Top**. Preparations for a wedding. Red-figure lebe. By the Painter of Athens. Classical Period. 420–410 B.C. Musée du Louvre. Paris, France. **Bottom.** Wedding scene (perhaps the wedding of Peleus and Thetis). Red-figure pyxis. By the Wedding Painter. Fifth century B.C. Musée du Louvre. Paris, France. **Page 12. Top.** Women spinning. Terra-cotta. Believed to be by the Diosphos Painter. Classical Greece. **Page 15. Left.** Seated young woman with her servant girl. Relief, funerary stele. 380–370 B.C. Karameikos, Greece. National Archaeological Museum, Athens. **Right.** Servant carrying an amphora full of water. Detail from black-figure lekythos (oil flask). Agora Museum, Athens. **Page 16. Right.** Tanagra female figure wearing a himation. Terra-cotta. Fourth century B.C. **Page 19.** The funeral banquet. Greek wall painting from the tomb of the diver. Early fifth century B.C. Museo Archeologico Nazionale. Paestum, Italy. **Page 20. Top.** School scene. Red-figure cup. By the Penthesilea Painter. 460–450 B.C. Musée du Louvre. Paris, France. **Bottom**. Man writing. Terra-cotta figurine. 520–480 B.C. Thebes, Greece. Musée du Louvre. Paris, France.

Web Sites

Due to the changing nature of Internet links, PowerKids Press has developed an online list of Web sites related to the subject of this book. This site is updated regularly. Please use this link to access the list:
www.powerkidslinks.com/psaciv/homegre/